New Cornish Cookbook

October 2nd 2004

Margaret Wilson

Tor Mark · Redruth

The Tor Mark Series

Ancient Cornwall
Birds of Cornwall
Birds of Devon
Charlestown
China clay
Classic Cornish ghost stories
Classic Devon ghost stories
Classic folk tales from the
  Land's End
Classic ghost stories from the
  Land's End
Classic West Country ghost stories
Cornish fairies
Cornish folklore
Cornish inventors
Cornish legends
Cornish mining – underground
Cornish mining industry
Cornish recipes
Cornish saints
Cornish seashore
Cornwall's engine houses
Cornwall's railways
Cornwall's history
Devon customs and superstitions
Devon legends

Devon seashore
Devonshire jokes and stories
Do you know Cornwall?
Fed fitty
Jan Bedella's fiddle
Introducing Cornwall
Lost ports of Cornwall
New Cornish cookbook
The pasty book
Shipwrecks around Land's End
Shipwrecks around the Lizard
Shipwrecks of North Devon
Shipwrecks on Cornwall's North
  coast
The story of the Cornish language
The story of St Ives
The story of Truro Cathedral
Strange tales of the Cornish coast
Tales of the Cornish smugglers
Twelve walks on the Lizard
Wildflowers of the Cornish coast
Wildflowers of the Devon coast
Wildflowers of the Cornish
  hedgerows
Wildflowers of the Devon
  hedgerows

Published by Tor Mark, PO Box 4, Redruth, Cornwall, TR16 5YX
First published 2002
© 2002 Margaret Wilson
ISBN 0-85025-395-0
The text illustrations are by Sue Lewington
Cover photographs by Andrew Besley
Printed in Great Britain by R Booth (The Troutbeck Press), Mabe, Penryn, Cornwall

Introduction

What I love about cooking is that you can lose yourself in your kitchen, with all your cherished utensils and favourite ingredients around you. For me, whether I'm making something for the family or for visitors to our restaurant, time spent preparing delicious food is never a chore at all – I get so much pleasure from seeing others tucking into the end result!

I also believe that one of the keys to tasty, simple meals is to use fresh, local and preferably organic ingredients. Here in the Southwest it's becoming much easier to find them, and I always cook with them whenever I possibly can. If you can locate similar sources near you, give them a try and see what a difference they can make to your own cooking.

I was born and brought up in Cornwall – both my mum and dad were from old Cornish families – so a few of the traditional recipes in this book hold special memories for me. My husband, Paul, is Cornish too, and it's thanks to his mum that I have such lovely baking recipes, a couple of which I've included here. But most of the recipes are ones I've created or adapted myself in recent years. I've been asked for them so often by people in the restaurant that I felt it was about time I put them into print. I now hope you enjoy making – and eating – them as much as we all do at Tinhay Mill.

Please note: throughout the book, unless otherwise stated, spoon measurements are always level and eggs are size 2. And remember not to mix imperial with metric measurements.

The front cover photograph shows the following dishes:
Cream of mussel, saffron and scrumpy soup (page 8), Pasties (page 19), Hot peppered Coverack smoked mackerel (page 8), Chocolate rum truffles (page 23), Strawberry and almond meringue gateau (page 24), Paul's Mum's saffron buns (page 25), and Brandy snap basket with Spicy organic pears (pages 27 and 39).

Starters

Red pepper, tomato and fresh basil soup

(serves 6)

1 onion (finely chopped)
1 clove of garlic (crushed)
4 red peppers (washed, deseeded and chopped)
225 g (8 oz) fresh ripe tomatoes (quartered)
1 red chilli (finely chopped) (optional)
3 tbsp fresh basil (chopped)
1 small pot natural yoghurt
600 ml (1 pt) vegetable stock
salt and freshly milled black pepper

Place all the ingredients, except the basil and yoghurt, in a saucepan and bring to the boil. Reduce the heat and simmer for 30 minutes. Purée in a blender and then push through a fine sieve. Return to a clean pan, heat, check the seasoning and serve, adding a teaspoon of yoghurt and some freshly chopped basil as garnish.

Terrine of three white fish

(serves 8)

In this recipe, the terrine is wrapped in crêpes and served with a lime and watercress mayonnaise.

225 g (8 oz) monkfish (boned, filleted and skinned)
225 g (8 oz) brill (boned, filleted and skinned)
225 g (8 oz) seabass (boned, filleted and skinned)
4 egg whites
275 ml ($1/2$ pt) double cream
$1/4$ tsp sea salt and $1/4$ tsp cayenne pepper
2 tbsp freshly squeezed lemon juice
2 bay leaves
8 crêpes (13 cm / 5 in diameter)

Place the fish in a food processor with the seasoning, and blend for 5 seconds. Add the egg whites and cream, and blend for a further 10 seconds – don't overblend, as the consistency needs to be a little coarse rather than smooth.

Lightly grease a 900 g (2 lb) loaf tin with butter, and line with six crêpes. Fill with the fish mixture and press it well into the corners. Tuck in all the overlapping crêpes and cover with the remaining two.

Put 2 fresh bay leaves on the top and cover with buttered parchment or greaseproof paper, and then wrap the whole tin in tin foil. Place in a bain marie (a deep roasting tin two-thirds filled with hot water) in the centre of the oven, and cook for an hour and a half at 180°C/350°F/gas mark 4.

Leave to cool, then refrigerate for at least four hours before serving (preferably make the terrine the day before you need it).

For the lime and watercress mayonnaise

2 size two egg yolks
1 small clove of crushed garlic (optional)
275 ml (1/2 pt) groundnut or olive oil
2 tbsp freshly squeezed lime juice
50 g (2 oz) fresh watercress
salt and freshly milled white pepper
1/2 tsp mustard powder
2 tbsp dry white wine

Place the egg yolks in a food processor with the salt, pepper, crushed garlic and mustard powder, and blend these together. Continue blending while slowly trickling in the oil – this takes two or three minutes.

When the sauce has thickened, add the water cress, lime juice and white wine, and mix well together. Check the seasoning. The mayonnaise should be of a coating consistency.

Cornish game soup

(serves 6)

450 g (1 lb) mixed game meat (cut into small pieces)
110 g (4 oz) swede (chopped)
110 g (4 oz) leeks (chopped)
110 g (4 oz) carrots (chopped)
110 g (4 oz) onions (chopped)
1 stick of celery (chopped)
1.5 l (2 1/2 pt) game stock (see opposite page)
1 tsp freshly chopped thyme
1 tsp freshly chopped sage
1 tsp freshly chopped parsley
1 clove of garlic (crushed)
salt and freshly milled black pepper
1 tbsp tomato purée
50 g (2 oz) butter
50 g (2 oz) plain flour
1 bay leaf (broken)

Place half the flour in a tray, season, and roll the game meat in the flour.

Melt the butter in a heavy bottomed pan and, when hot, sauté a third of the meat at a time, keeping it moving so that it browns evenly. Drain with a slotted spoon.

Next, put all the meat back in the pan, and over a gentle heat stir in the remaining flour, tomato purée and garlic.

Cook for 2 minutes before pouring in a little stock at a time, stirring continuously. Add the vegetables and herbs, bring to the boil and then turn to a low heat.

Gently simmer with the lid on for 1 1/4 hours, stirring every 15 minutes. When cooked, take off the heat, adjust the seasoning and serve in hot bowls with freshly baked bread.

Garnish with chopped parsley.

For the game stock
(makes approximately 1.5 l (2 $^1/_2$ pt))

900g (2 lb) mixed game bones
1 bay leaf
sprig of thyme
3 or 4 parsley stalks
1 tsp whole black peppercorns
1 carrot (chopped)
1 celery stick (chopped)
1 medium red onion (chopped)
2.25 l (4 pt) cold water

Place the bones and vegetables on a large baking tray in a preheated oven (220°C/425°F/gas mark 7) and brown evenly for 25–30 minutes – you'll need to turn them to make sure they don't burn. Remove from the oven and place in a large pan with the remaining ingredients. Bring to the boil, then turn the heat down to simmer and cook for 3 $^1/_2$ to 4 hours. Strain through a very fine sieve or muslin, and allow to cool. Your stock can be frozen or kept in the fridge for up to 3 days.

Hot peppered Coverack smoked mackerel

(serves 4)

Served with lemon and lavender jelly (see page 37), this dish makes an excellent starter and takes only a few minutes to prepare and cook.

4 x 150 g (6 oz) smoked mackerel fillets
1 tbsp finely crushed black peppercorns
25 g (2 oz) unsalted butter
2 tbsp lemon and lavender jelly (see page 37)
1 tbsp freshly chopped dill

Prepare the smoked mackerel by taking off the skin. Then smother the under side of each with the crushed black peppers. Melt the butter gently in a pan and add the fillets. As the fish is already cooked, it's just a matter of heating it through for about 2 minutes each side. Make sure the heat is gentle to keep the mackerel moist: if you cook it too fiercely or quickly it will dry up. Once heated through, add the jelly to the pan and let it dissolve and be absorbed into the fillets – this takes 30 seconds. Sprinkle with dill and serve on a crispy salad.

Cream of mussel, saffron and scrumpy soup

(serves 6)

700 g (1 1/2 lb) fresh mussels (washed and bearded)
110 g (4 oz) onions (finely chopped)
110 g (4 oz) leeks (finely chopped)
1 tsp freshly chopped thyme
1 tsp freshly chopped parsley
110 g (4 oz) fennel bulb (finely chopped)
1 celery stalk (finely chopped)
2 cloves of garlic (crushed)
1 pinch of saffron (buy from a local health food shop for a much better flavour)
570 ml (1 pt) fish stock (see opposite page)

275 ml (^{1}/$_2$ pt) scrumpy
25 g (1 oz) plain flour
50 g (2 oz) butter
140 ml (^{1}/$_4$ pt) double cream
salt and freshly milled black pepper

Melt the butter in a pan over a low heat and sauté the onions, fennel, crushed garlic, celery and leeks until soft and without colour. Stir in the flour and cook gently for 2 minutes. Then gradually add the scrumpy, fish stock, saffron, mussels and herbs. Bring to the boil and simmer for 5 minutes. Liquidise the soup and strain through a fine sieve into a clean pan. Add the cream, adjust the seasoning and serve.

For the fish stock [makes 1.2 l (2 pt)]

1 large onion (sliced)
1 stick of celery (chopped)
1 fresh bay leaf
6 whole peppercorns
675 g (1^1/$_2$ lb) white fish bones
3 or 4 parsley stalks
1 carrot (chopped)
1 leek (chopped)
pinch of salt
1 l (1^3/$_4$ pt) water
275 ml (^{1}/$_2$ pt) dry white wine or dry cider

Put everything into a large saucepan, bring to the boil, turn the heat to very low and leave to simmer for 20 minutes. Allow the stock to cool before straining it through muslin. It will keep for up to 2 days in the fridge, or you can freeze it for a month.

Main courses

Filo baskets filled with leeks, red peppers and courgettes

(serves 4)

A filo pastry case flavoured with garlic, filled with red peppers, leeks, courgettes and goat's cheese, and served with tomato and red pepper sauce.

> 4 x 7.5 cm (3 in) ramekin dishes (use up-side down)
> 110 g (4 oz) melted butter and 1 crushed clove of garlic (optional)
> 4 x 25 cm (10 in) square sheets of filo pastry

Preheat the oven to 180°C/350°F/gas mark 4. Cut each sheet of pastry into four 13 cm (5 in) squares. Brush one side of the squares with melted garlic butter and place four squares (butter side down) onto each of the up-side-down ramekin dishes – with the last squares, brush on both sides. Put on a baking tray and bake for 8–10 minutes or until golden brown. Leave to cool for just a few minutes before gently lifting the baskets (they are quite fragile) off the ramekins onto a wire rack.

For the tomato and red pepper sauce

> 2 large red peppers (roasted, skinned and finely chopped)
> 1 large onion (chopped finely)
> 1 clove of garlic (crushed)
> 450 g (1 lb) very ripe tomatoes (blanched, skinned and chopped)
> 1 tbsp mild olive oil
> 1 tbsp soy sauce
> 1 tbsp dark muscovado sugar

Heat the oil, add the onions and sweat them until they begin to caramelise – this usually takes 10 minutes. Add the crushed garlic and stir in the sugar and soy sauce. Lastly, put in the tomatoes and peppers, and leave to simmer gently for approximately 10 minutes.

The sauce is now ready to serve.

If you want to spice the sauce up some more, add the following ingredients as the onions begin to caramelise:

$^{1}/_{4}$ tsp ground cumin

$^{1}/_{4}$ tsp ground coriander

$^{1}/_{4}$ tsp chilli powder

For the filo filling

225 g (8 oz) blanched leeks (sliced)

225 g (8 oz) red peppers (roasted and skinned)

225 g (8 oz) courgettes (washed and chopped)

2 cloves of garlic (crushed)

110 g (4 oz) goat's cheese

275 ml ($^{1}/_{2}$ pt) double cream

25 g (1 oz) butter (melted)

1 tbsp mild olive oil

basil leaves to decorate

On a medium heat melt the butter in a sauté pan until it bubbles. Then add the olive oil – this should prevent the butter burning. Add the courgettes and cook until golden. Lower the heat before putting in the garlic, roasted peppers, blanched leeks and cream. Gently cook together for 1–2 minutes until the mixture thickens, then take off the heat and stir in the goat's cheese.

To assemble the whole dish: warm a filo case, pour 3 tablespoons of the sauce onto a hot plate and then put the filo case on top. Fill with the vegetables and cheese, and decorate with fresh basil before serving.

Pork butterfly ribs glazed with a ginger sauce

(serves 4)

This recipe also works well as a starter.

4 x 175 g (6 oz) pork butterfly ribs (or loin chops – ask your
   butcher if you're not sure)
4 tbsp dark soy sauce
110 g (4 oz) caster sugar
a cube (2.5 cm / 1 in) of fresh ginger (crushed)
4 spring onions
1 l (1 ^{3}/$_4$ pt) water
4 tbsp dry sherry

Place the ribs in a shallow pan with all the ingredients except the
sugar and the spring onions. Bring to the boil and simmer for 45
minutes with the lid on. Then drain the ribs and put them in an
ovenproof dish, keeping them hot while you reduce the liquor.

Pour the liquid back into the pan, add the sugar and boil rapidly
for about 15 minutes until the sauce is reduced to a coating glaze –
it will darken as it thickens.

Arrange the ribs, cover with the sauce and add the spring onions.
Serve as a starter with freshly baked bread and a crispy salad or as a
main course with vegetables.

Rack of lamb served with poached plums and a madeira and rosemary sauce

(serves 4)

1 pair best end of lamb (French trimmed), to give 12 cutlets (ask
   your butcher to do this for you and make sure you have
   enough trimmings and bones for your stock)
salt and freshly milled black pepper
2 tbsp olive oil for brushing
8 fresh sprigs of rosemary, plus extra for garnish

For the lamb stock

1 kg (2 lb 2 oz) lean lamb trimmings and bones (no fat)
6 shallots (chopped)
2 carrots (chopped)
2 sticks celery (chopped)
2 whole cloves of garlic
a few parsley stalks
sprig of fresh thyme
1 tsp whole black peppercorns
1.2 l (2 pt) cold water

Begin by making the stock. Only half is needed for this recipe, so you can freeze the rest for another time – believe me, once you have made good stock, it's worth hanging on to!

Place the trimmings, bones, vegetables, herbs, garlic and peppercorns into a roasting pan in a preheated oven (200°C / 400°F / gas mark 6) for 25 minutes or until golden brown. Transfer to a large saucepan, add the water and bring to the boil. Turn down low and leave gently simmering for two hours. Skim off any scum as it rises to the surface by straining through a fine sieve or muslin.

For the poached plums

6 Victoria plums (cut into halves and stoned)
1 tbsp caster sugar
150 ml (5 fl oz) water

Place all the ingredients into a pan and simmer over a medium heat for approximately 8–10 minutes until the plums are cooked but still firm.

For the madeira and rosemary sauce

2 sprigs of rosemary
75 ml (3 fl oz) madeira
50 g (2 oz) unsalted butter
275 ml ($1/2$ pt) lamb stock

To cook the lamb and sauce

Preheat the oven to 200°C/400°F/gas mark 6. Brush the lamb with the olive oil, season and place in a roasting pan with the sprigs of rosemary. Cook for 15 minutes – the meat will be pink and tender.

While the meat is in the oven, reduce the stock by half by boiling rapidly. Then take the lamb out and put on a preheated serving dish to rest, keeping it hot while you make the sauce.

For the sauce, first deglaze the meat pan with the madeira, scraping up all the juices. Then add the reduced stock and a sprig of rosemary. Pour into a saucepan and reduce by half. Season to taste, and whisk in the butter a little at a time to thicken your sauce and give it a glossy finish. Strain through a fine sieve.

Cut the lamb into three cutlets per person, criss-crossing the bones, and serve on warmed plates with the plums and sauce, and sprigs of rosemary for garnish.

Suet potato cake

(serves 6)

This potato cake is crispy, and complements roast lamb with mint sauce beautifully.

225 g (8 oz) self-raising flour
110 g (4 oz) suet
450 g (1 lb) raw potato (grated)
salt and milled black pepper

In a mixing bowl sift the flour and salt, add the suet and black pepper. Grate in the potato and mix together until a soft dough forms (you should have enough liquid from the potato without having to add any extra). Leave to rest for 5 minutes.

Grease a deep sandwich tin (15 x 4 cm/6 x 1^1/$_2$ in), and then shape your potato cake with your hands to almost the size of the tin. Place it in the tin and push the sides evenly into the remaining space. Bake for 45 minutes at 200°C/400°F/gas mark 6.

Chicken pie with herby rough puff pastry

1.35 kg (3 lb) fresh chicken (diced into 2.5 cm / 1 in cubes and
    coated in 75 g / 3 oz of seasoned flour)
1 tbsp freshly chopped parsley
1 tbsp freshly chopped sage
110 g (4 oz) shallots (finely chopped)
110 g (4 oz) leeks (finely chopped, blanched in 150 ml / 5 fl oz
    boiling water for 2 minutes and then strained)
1 packet of saffron (healthfood shops often offer better quality,
    cheaper selections)
3 tbsp dry cider
275 ml ($1/2$ pt) double cream
75 g (3 oz) butter
1 tbsp olive oil
$1/2$ tsp salt
$1/2$ tsp freshly milled white pepper

Heat the cider until it almost boils, and pour into a basin with the saffron. Allow to stand for 10 minutes.

In the meantime, heat 25 g (1 oz) of the butter in a sauté pan, add the shallots and cook them for 3–4 minutes without colour.

In a wok or large sauté pan heat the remaining butter with the olive oil, and seal the diced seasoned chicken by browning evenly (don't try doing too much at a time).

Place in a large saucepan with the shallots, strained leeks, parsley, sage, cider and saffron, and add the salt and pepper.

Stir everything together and gently bring to the boil. Take off the heat and stir in the double cream. Transfer to a 1.5 l ($2 1/2$ pt) round or oval pie dish with a rim.

For the pastry, follow the recipe on page 19, adding $1/2$ tsp each of chopped parsley, thyme and sage with the butter to the flour and salt.

Roll out the pastry to a thickness of 5 mm ($1/4$ in). Cut a strip, egg wash it and place it around the rim of the dish. Egg wash the upper side of the strip before putting the rest of the rolled out pastry over the mixture. Trim the edge and, using your thumb and a knife, make a fluted edge. Egg wash the top of the pie, and cook in a pre-heated oven (190°C/375°F/gas mark 5) for 45 minutes.

Rabbit casserole

(serves 4)

> 1 rabbit (cut into three joints)
> soak in 1.2 l (2 pt) of water and 2 tbsp salt for 2–3 hours
> 50 g (2 oz) seasoned cornflour ($1/4$ tsp cayenne pepper and
> $1/2$ tsp salt)
> 225 g (8 oz) carrots (chopped)
> 225 g (8 oz) onions (chopped)
> 225 g (8 oz) leeks (chopped)
> 1 stick of celery (chopped)
> 2 tbsp freshly chopped parsley
> 1 tsp freshly chopped thyme
> 2 fresh bay leaves
> 1 tbsp olive oil
> 75 g (3 oz) butter (unsalted)
> 1 large cooking apple (chopped)
> 150 ml ($1/4$ pt) dry cider

After soaking the rabbit, drain it off and wash in cold water. Pat dry with some kitchen paper and dredge in seasoned cornflour.

Heat the oil and the butter in a large pan, then brown each joint of the rabbit on both sides. Place into your casserole dish, adding the prepared vegetables and chopped apple, bay leaves, thyme and parsley.

Cover with 725 ml ($1 1/4$ pt) cold water and the cider, and transfer to the centre shelf of the oven. Cook at 200°C/400°F/gas mark 6 for 2 to $2 1/2$ hours.

Scallops with Cornish smoked bacon

(serves 4)

For this delightful recipe, the scallops and bacon are cooked in a brie and cream sauce and served in filo baskets.

4 filo baskets (see page 10)
16 large scallops with the coral left on (cleaned and trimmed)
4 slices of rindless smoked back bacon (grilled and chopped)
110 g (4 oz) St Endellion brie (diced)
110 g (4 oz) bulb fennel (chopped and sautéd)
10 g ($^1/_2$ oz) butter
10 g ($^1/_2$ oz) flour
275 ml ($^1/_2$ pt) fish stock (see page 9)
150 ml ($^1/_4$ pt) double cream
olive oil
1 tsp chopped parsley

Have dinner plates and filo baskets in a warming oven, ready to assemble the dish.

Place a heavy frying pan or skillet on a high heat with the butter and a few drops of olive oil. When it is sizzling but not brown, put the scallops in and cook for just 30 seconds each side. Transfer to a warm oven.

Add the flour to the pan and cook for a few seconds, then pour in the fish stock, slowly whisking all the time. Take off the heat, add the diced brie and put back onto a low heat.

Pour in the cream and gently bring back to the boil before putting through a fine sieve. Keep hot.

To assemble the dish, place the filo baskets on warm plates. Drop four scallops, a little bacon and fennel into each basket, cover with the sauce, sprinkle with chopped parsley, and serve with a crispy salad and some Cornish new potatoes.

Turnip and bacon pasty

(makes 4 pasties)

For the short crust pastry

450 g (1 lb) plain flour (sifted)
pinch of salt
75 g (3 oz) lard
75 g (3 oz) margarine
115 ml (4 fl oz) water

Make the pastry by rubbing the fats into the sifted flour and salt until the mixture resembles fine breadcrumbs. Create a well in the centre and mix in the cold water. Knead together gently into a firm ball, cover in cling film and put in the fridge for 20 minutes.

For the filling

450 g (1 lb) turnip (diced)
450 g (1 lb) chopped lean Cornish bacon (smoked or green)
2 tbsp freshly chopped parsley
salt and freshly ground white pepper
50 g (2 oz) unsalted butter
1 beaten egg with a little milk for brushing the pastry

Line a baking tray with parchment paper, and preheat the oven to 200°C/400°F/gas mark 6. In a large bowl mix the turnip, chopped parsley, bacon and seasoning. Roll out the pastry and cut into 4 rings, each approximately 13 cm (5 in) in diameter. Brush each around the edge with the egg wash, and divide the mixture and butter among the rings, placing them in the centre.

Bring the edges of the pastry together, crimp or press firmly, and place on the lined baking tray. Put in the preheated oven on the top shelf. After 30 minutes the pasties should be golden brown in colour. Turn the oven down to 180°C/350°F/gas mark 4, cover the pasties with foil to prevent further browning and put them on the centre shelf for another 30 minutes to finish cooking. They make superb picnic treats.

Traditional Cornish pasty

(makes 4 good sized pasties)

This is grandmother's pasty recipe. She taught all her children to cook, including the boys. My Uncle Henry, who celebrated his 80th birthday this year, still makes his own pasties. (Some people prefer short crust pastry (see p. 18), so try both and decide for yourself!)

For the rough puff pastry

225 g (8 oz) plain flour
175 g (6 oz) Cornish butter (cubed and chilled)
pinch of salt
1 tsp freshly squeezed lemon juice
approx. 115 ml (4 fl oz) ice-cold water

Sift the flour and salt into a large mixing bowl, and add the cubed butter. Make a well in the centre and pour in the lemon juice and water. Mix to a soft dough without crushing the butter, then wrap in cling film and put in the fridge for 20 minutes to rest.

Flour a board and roll your pastry into an oblong shape approximately 12 mm ($^1/_2$ in) thick. Keeping the corners square, fold the top third down towards you and the bottom third up. Give the pastry one turn so that the folds are on the left and right, and roll again. Repeat the folding procedure, and roll one more time.

Wrap in cling film again and put back in the fridge until you are ready to use it.

For the filling

350 g (12 oz) beef skirt (chopped small)
350 g (12 oz) potatoes (chopped small)
110 g (4 oz) onions (chopped small)
110 g (4 oz) swede (chopped small)
1 tsp ground white pepper and 1 tsp salt
25 g (1 oz) butter (cut into four)
2 tbsp freshly chopped parsley (optional)
1 beaten egg for glazing

In a large mixing bowl place the meat, potatoes, onions and swede, and add the seasoning and, if you're using it, the parsley. Mix well – the best way to do this is with your hands.

Flour a board, roll out the pastry to a thickness of 3 mm (1/8 in) and cut into four rounds measuring 21 cm (8 1/2 in). Egg wash all round the edges of the circles. Then divide the filling into four equal amounts and place on the pastry, adding a knob of butter to each pasty. Bring the pastry together, crimp or press firmly together with your thumb and forefinger, and brush with egg glaze.

Cook at 200°C/400°F/gas mark 6 on a baking tray lined with parchment paper for 1 hour 15 minutes. Start off on the top shelf and after the first 30 minutes, or when the pasties are golden brown in colour, cover with tin foil and move to the centre shelf for the rest of the cooking time. Serve straight from the oven or, if preferred, serve cold with Fiery green tomato chutney (see page 36).

Beef and egg pie in suet crust pastry

(serves 6)

For the pastry

225 g (8 oz) self-raising flour
110 g (4 oz) shredded suet
110 g (4 oz) raw potato (grated)
1 tbsp freshly chopped thyme
1 egg (beaten)
3 tbsp cold water
salt and 1/2 tsp freshly milled black pepper
egg wash (1 beaten egg)

Sift the flour and salt into a mixing bowl, and add the suet, thyme and black pepper. Grate the potato into the flour mixture, and add the egg and water. Mix to a soft dough. Leave to rest for 10 minutes. Flour a board, roll out the suet dough and line a round 20 cm (8 in) sandwich tin 4 cm (1 1/2 in) deep. Trim, leaving a little overlapping the edge of the tin.

For the filling

350 g (12 oz) skirt (cut into 1 cm / 1 / 2 in cubes)
110 g (4 oz) onions (chopped)
6 eggs (beaten)
1 / 2 tsp salt
1 / 2 tsp ground white pepper

Fill the pastry with the chopped beef and onions, and pour in the beaten eggs. Sprinkle evenly with the salt and pepper, and egg wash the overlapping pastry. Roll the rest of the pastry and cover the filling. Press down and seal the edge with your thumb. Trim, egg wash the pastry, and place the pie on a baking tray. Cook for 1 hour at 200°C / 400°F / gas mark 6.

Welsh rarebit with beefy tomatoes

(serves 4)

Manallack Farmhouse is a Cornish cheese made on the Lizard Peninsula. A good substitute would be Cheshire cheese.

4 beef tomatoes (halved around the middle and deseeded)
225 g (8 oz) Manallack Farmhouse cheese (grated)
2 size 2 egg yolks
1 tsp English mustard (made up)
2 tbsp Cornish beer
pinch of cayenne pepper
1 heaped tsp freshly chopped parsley

Preheat the oven to 190°C / 375°F / gas mark 5. First place the prepared tomatoes on a baking tray. Next, mix all the other ingredients together in a bowl until everything is well incorporated. Then fill the tomato halves and pop in the oven for 10 minutes or until golden.

You can also make this recipe with field mushrooms for a tasty snack, or add grilled Cornish bacon for a great breakfast.

Puddings

Viv's gooey chocolate pudding

This recipe was kindly given to me by our head waitress, Viv, whose grandmother passed it down to her. It makes:

12 individual puddings (in dariole moulds – cooking time
35–40 minutes) OR
1 tray bake (37 x 27 cm / 14 1/2 x 10 1/2 in – cooking time
35–40 minutes OR
1 cake (20 cm / 8 in square – cooking time 50–60 minutes)

350 g (12 oz) self-raising flour
400 g (14 oz) caster sugar
110 g (4 oz) cocoa powder
200 g (7 oz) soft margarine
2 eggs
1 tsp bicarbonate of soda
1 tsp salt
2 tsp baking powder
4 tsp coffee powder in 330 ml (12 fl oz) boiling water

Preheat the oven to 170°C / 325°F / gas mark 3. If using a tray bake or cake tin, line with parchment, or if using moulds, grease lightly with lard or margarine. Place everything except the coffee in a mixer and blend together on a slow speed. When well blended, slowly pour in the coffee and mix slowly until smooth. You may think the mixture is too runny, but don't worry as this texture is what makes the pudding/cake so light. When it is cooked it will feel firm – try the skewer test: if it comes out clean, whatever you've made is ready.

The cake is suitable as a celebration cake and can be iced with chocolate fudge. The tray bake can be served with a fondant icing sprinkled with pecan nuts or flaked almonds.

The pudding is fabulous served with hot chocolate sauce.

For the chocolate sauce

225g (8oz) plain good quality chocolate
1 tbsp coffee powder
4 tbsp boiling water
75ml (3 fl oz) double cream

Place a bowl over a pan of simmering water. Break the chocolate into pieces, put in the bowl and melt for 2–3 minutes. Meanwhile dissolve the coffee in the boiling water. When the chocolate has melted, take the bowl off the saucepan, add the hot coffee, and whisk until smooth and shiny. Leave to cool for 5 minutes and then whisk in the double cream, and serve. If the sauce starts to solidify, just place it over the pan of simmering water for a few minutes.

Chocolate rum truffles coated in pecan nuts

275ml ($^{1}/_{2}$ pt) double cream
2 tbsp dark rum (optional)
275g (10oz) good quality plain chocolate
75g (3oz) unsalted butter
75g (3oz) pecan nuts (roasted and crushed)

Melt the chocolate in a bowl over a saucepan of simmering water. In another saucepan bring the cream to the boil, then add to the melted chocolate, stirring until it is well incorporated. Chop the butter into small pieces and mix this into the chocolate mixture as well until it dissolves. Lastly, add the rum and leave to cool. Then put in the fridge until solid.

Meanwhile place the pecan nuts on a baking tray in a preheated oven (180°C/350°F/gas mark 4) and roast for around 15 minutes – check them frequently. When they are roasted, take them out of the oven and leave them to cool before crushing them lightly.

For the next stage you'll need cold hands! Take half a teaspoon of mixture, roll it into a ball, and then roll it in the crushed pecan nuts until it is coated evenly. Put each truffle into a petit four case and pop on a tray back in the fridge until you wish to serve them.

Strawberry and almond meringue gateau

(serves 6)

For the meringue

150 g (5 oz) ground almonds
185 g (6 1/2 oz) caster sugar
5 egg whites (size 2)
275 ml (1/2 pt) double cream (whipped)

For filling and decoration

350 g (12 oz) strawberries (washed, hulled and sliced)
peppermint leaves
6 uniform whole strawberries

Line a baking tray (30 x 45 cm / 12 x 18 in) with parchment paper and preheat the oven to 180°C / 350°F / gas mark 4.

Beat the egg whites until stiff peaks form, then add 150 g (5 oz) sugar a tablespoon at a time and whisk at full speed for 3–4 minutes until it has dissolved. Fold in the remaining sugar and ground almonds. Spread evenly onto the baking tray and bake in the oven for 20–25 minutes or until it is crisp and golden brown. Leave to cool for just a few minutes only, as it is important to cut out the circles while the meringue is still warm. Using a 7.5 cm (3 in) pastry cutter, cut into 18 circles. Leave until completely cold, and in the meantime make the coulis.

For the strawberry coulis

225 g (8 oz) strawberries (washed, hulled and sliced)
25 g (1 oz) icing sugar
2 tbsp freshly squeezed lemon juice
1 tbsp cold water

Place all the ingredients into a food processor and blend for 30 seconds. Strain through a very fine sieve.

To assemble the dessert, you will need six 20 cm (8 in) dessert plates. For each, cover the bottom with the coulis. Next, take three meringue circles: pipe cream around the edge of two of them and evenly spread with sliced strawberries. Place one on top of the other. Finally, put the third circle on top of the first two, pipe a whirl of cream in the centre and decorate with a fantail or a whole strawberry, some peppermint leaves and, if you can get hold of them, borage flowers. Dust with icing sugar and serve.

Chocolate and coffee liqueur ice cream loaf
(serves 8)

225 g (8 oz) caster sugar
8 egg yolks (size 2)
275 ml ($^1/_2$ pt) double cream
275 ml ($^1/_2$ pt) full cream milk
110 g (4 oz) plain chocolate
225 g (8 oz) mascarpone cream cheese
2 tsp strong black coffee

Pour the cream and milk into a 1.2 litre (2 pint) saucepan, and bring to the boil. Meanwhile whisk the egg yolks and sugar together for approximately 5 minutes until light and creamy. Add the heated liquid to the mixture at the slowest speed possible until everything is well incorporated.

Put the custard back into the saucepan on a very gentle heat, stirring all the time until it starts to thicken – this should take only 2–3 minutes (if you over-heat, you'll end up with very expensive sweetened scrambled eggs). Take off the heat, and pass through a fine sieve.

Melt the chocolate in a basin on the top of a saucepan of hot water. Then add the dissolved coffee and whisk in two-thirds of your ice-cream custard. Cover with muslin or a clean tea towel and leave to cool. Once cooled, churn the chocolate custard in an ice-cream maker for about 20 minutes for a smooth and velvety finish. Spoon it into a 900 g (2 lb) loaf tin lined with parchment, cover with parchment paper and put in the freezer.

Add the mascarpone cheese to the remaining custard and give it a good whisk for a smooth, creamy consistency. Then churn for 20 minutes, as before. Take the parchment paper off, and place the custard on top of the chocolate ice cream. Cover with parchment paper and cling film and put back into the freezer – it needs to be frozen for at least 2 hours before cutting into slices and serving.

For the coffee liqueur and cream sauce

    2 egg yolks
    25 g (1 oz) caster sugar
    150 ml (¹/₄ pt) double cream
    150 ml (¹/₄ pt) full cream milk
    1 tbsp freshly ground coffee (or filter coffee)
    2 tbsp coffee liqueur (such as Kahlua)

Beat the egg yolks and sugar together until you have a pale, thick and creamy consistency. Place the cream, coffee and milk into a saucepan and bring to the boil. Pass through a fine sieve – some of the coffee grains will escape, but this will just add to the flavour. Then beat on a slow speed into the egg and sugar mixture.

Next, put back into the saucepan on a very low heat for 2–3 minutes, stirring all the time until the mixture thickens. Pour into a cold bowl and leave to cool. When completely cold, add the coffee liqueur and serve with the ice cream.

Brandy snap baskets

You can fill these baskets with ice cream or fruit, and dust with a little icing sugar.

  110 g (4 oz) butter
  110 g (4 oz) syrup
  110 g (4 oz) caster sugar
  110 g (4 oz) plain flour
  grated rind of 1 orange

Preheat the oven to 170°C/325°F/gas mark 3 and line a baking tin with parchment paper.

In a saucepan melt the butter with the syrup and sugar until the sugar has dissolved. Take off the heat and leave to cool for a few minutes, then add the sifted flour and orange rind.

Roll two balls from the mixture, each weighing about 10 g ($^1/_2$ oz), and place one towards either end of the tray – make sure there is sufficient space between and around them to prevent them running in to each other or the sides of the tray while cooking.

Put in the oven for approximately 8 minutes until golden brown in colour – make sure you have two juice glasses (around 5 cm/2 in wide) turned upside down, ready for when they come out of the oven.

Take the snaps off the tray but keep them on the paper and leave to cool for a few seconds or until the edges are firming up. Then whip them off the parchment and place them over the glasses, straight away moulding into the shape of lacy baskets. When completely cold, take them off the glasses and place on a wire rack. Repeat the procedure until you have used all the mixture.

If you like the idea of chocolate baskets, use 75 g (3 oz) plain flour and 25 g (1 oz) cocoa powder.

Bramble mousse with bramble sauce

3 egg yolks
275 ml (¹/₂ pt) milk
110 g (4 oz) caster sugar
450 g (1 lb) blackberries
4 leaves of gelatine
275 ml (¹/₂ pt) double cream
2 tsp lemon juice
2 tsp kirsch
mint leaves, a few extra blackberries and icing sugar
    for decoration

On a low heat place the blackberries, 55 g (2 oz) sugar and the lemon juice in a heavy-based saucepan and gently heat to release the juices. After 5 minutes, take off the heat and liquidise. Strain through a nylon sieve or muslin.

Meanwhile beat the egg yolks and remaining sugar, and bring the milk to the boil. Add the boiling milk slowly to the egg mixture and stir. Then put into another heavy-based saucepan and cook over a low heat, stirring all the time until the mixture coats the back of your spoon – this usually takes about 5 minutes.

Cover the gelatine leaves with cold water for a few minutes until they resemble jelly, after which drain off the water and mix the gelatine into the hot custard. Whisk for a few seconds until it has completely dissolved, and then strain through a sieve into a clean, cold bowl.

When the custard is cold, whip the cream – don't overwhip – and fold it in. Mix with half the bramble syrup, pour into small moulds and put in the fridge for at least 2 hours. Then turn each mousse onto a plate, pour over some of the remaining syrup and decorate with mint leaves and spare blackberries. Dust with a little icing sugar and serve with clotted cream.

Cakes and biscuits

Cherry, date and banana tea bread

A delicious moist tea bread served with or without butter.

225 g (8 oz) self-raising flour
3/4 tsp cinnamon
110 g (4 oz) caster sugar
110 g (4 oz) unsalted butter
1 tbsp honey
110 g (4 oz) chopped glacé cherries
juice and rind of 1 lemon and 1 orange
125 g (4 1/2 oz) chopped dates
2 eggs
450 g (1 lb) ripe bananas

Line a 900 g (2 lb) loaf tin with parchment paper, making sure the paper extends 5 cm (2 in) beyond the top of the tin, and preheat the oven to 175°C / 360°F / gas mark 4.

Sift the flour and cinnamon into a mixing bowl, rub in the butter, and add the sugar, chopped cherries, dates and lemon and orange rind. Pulp the bananas in a food processor with the fruit juices, honey and eggs, and pour the mixture onto the dry ingredients. Mix everything together well, then transfer to the prepared tin and bake for 80–90 minutes. Test the loaf with a skewer – if it comes out clean, your loaf is ready; if it's a little sticky, leave for a further 10 minutes. Remove from the oven and allow to cool before taking out of the tin and placing on a wire rack. When cold, wrap in tin foil and store in the fridge.

Heavy buns

My husband Paul remembers his mother making these every week, along with her saffron buns (see page 35).

450 g (1 lb) self-raising flour
110 g (4 oz) margarine
110 g (4 oz) lard
50 g (2 oz) caster sugar
pinch of salt
350 g (12 oz) currants
150 ml (5 fl oz) milk
grated rind and juice of 1 lemon

Sift the flour and salt into a mixing bowl. Rub in the lard, and add the sugar, fruit and milk. Mix to a soft dough, and roll out on a floured board into a strip approximately 15 cm (6 in) wide. Place half the margarine in small pieces over the bottom two thirds of the mixture. Fold over the top third without any margarine, and then fold the bottom third over this. Give half a turn so that the folds are at the sides.

Roll out again into a thin strip and spread the remaining margarine, as before, repeating the folding procedure. Finally roll to a thickness of 1 cm ($^1/_2$ in) and cut with a biscuit cutter. Put on a greased baking sheet and brush with egg wash. Bake at 200°C/ 400°F/ gas mark 6 for 15–20 minutes.

Oak smoked cheese scones
(makes 12)

The special cheese used in this recipe is made just outside Launceston and is called Tala Smoked, but you could substitute any good smoked Cheddar cheese. The scones are at their best served warm straight from the oven with lashings of butter.

225 g (8 oz) self-raising flour
2 tsp baking powder
1 tsp English mustard powder
$1/4$ tsp cayenne pepper
$1/2$ tsp salt
50 g (2 oz) butter or margarine
110 g (4 oz) Tala Smoked cheese (grated)
1 egg
a little milk

Preheat the oven to 200°C/400°F/gas mark 6.

Sift the flour, baking powder, mustard and seasoning into a bowl. Rub in the butter and grated cheese. Then mix in the beaten egg and a little milk until a soft dough forms. Roll gently on a floured board to a thickness of 2.5 cm (1 in) and cut into scones with a 5 cm (2 in) pastry cutter. Place them onto a greased baking tray and put on the top shelf of the oven for approximately 10 minutes.

Organic digestive biscuits

(makes 24)

175g (6oz) organic wholemeal flour
50g (2oz) fine organic oatmeal
1 tsp baking powder
1/4 tsp salt
50g (2oz) organic light soft brown sugar
110g (4oz) butter (chopped)
4 tbsp milk

Preheat the oven to 180°C/350°F/gas mark 4. Place all the dry ingredients in a large mixing bowl, then rub in the chopped butter. Add the milk and mix into a soft ball. Wrap in cling film and leave to rest in the fridge for 10 minutes. Roll out onto a lightly floured board to a thickness of 3mm (1/8 in). Cut into 7.5cm (3in) biscuit shapes, place on a baking sheet lined with parchment paper, and bake for 10–15 minutes. Transfer to a wire rack and leave to cool.

Launceston cake

My mother used to make this cake, following an old Cornish recipe, and it was always absolutely delicious. Apart from adding a couple of extra ingredients – cherries and freshly grated lemon rind – I have left an often tried and tested recipe well alone!

225g (8oz) self-raising flour
175g (6oz) margarine
175g (6oz) caster sugar
50g (2oz) ground almonds
3 eggs
450g (1lb) currants
50g (2oz) candied lemon peel (chopped)
1/2 tbsp black treacle and 1 tbsp golden syrup
juice and rind of 1 lemon
50g (2oz) chopped cherries (optional)

Start by greasing and lining a 20 cm (8 in) round cake tin. Cream the margarine and sugar together until light and fluffy. Add the syrup and treacle, and then the eggs one at a time. Finally add all the remaining ingredients carefully into the mixture, making sure everything is incorporated. Bake for $1^1/_2$ to $1^3/_4$ hours on the centre shelf at 170°C/325°F/gas mark 3.

Apple juice and cinnamon boiled cake

225 g (8 oz) Cornish butter
150 ml (5 fl oz) cold water
150 ml (5 fl oz) pure apple juice
225 g (8 oz) muscovado sugar
175 g (6 oz) chopped dates
110 g (4 oz) chopped dried apricots
110 g (4 oz) chopped glacé cherries
225 g (8 oz) sultanas
450 g (1 lb) self-raising flour
2 tsp ground cinnamon
4 eggs (beaten)

Line two 900 g (2 lb) loaf tins with parchment paper.

Place all the ingredients, except the flour, cinnamon and eggs, into a large saucepan, and gently bring to the boil. Simmer for 5 minutes, stirring occasionally. Take off the heat and leave to cool – approximately 20 minutes.

Next, mix in the beaten eggs and fold in the sifted flour and cinnamon. Turn into the prepared tins and bake for $1^1/_4$ hours at 170°C/325°F/gas mark 4.

Leave to rest in the tins until quite cool before turning out onto a wire rack.

Deep tin apple and almond tarts

(makes 12)

These tarts are wonderful served hot with custard or cold with an afternoon cup of tea.

175 g (6 oz) plain flour
50g (2 oz) ground almonds
pinch of salt
110 g (4 oz) butter
25 g (1 oz) caster sugar
1 egg yolk
3 tbsp cold water
175 g (6 oz) apple purée

Sieve the flour and salt into a bowl, add the ground almonds and sugar, and rub in the butter gently through your fingers and thumbs without completely crushing it. Add the egg yolk and water, and mix with a fork until a ball forms. Wrap in cling film and place in the fridge for 30 minutes to rest.

Grease deep tart tins with lard and then roll out your pastry on a floured board. Aim for a thickness of 3 mm ($1/8$ in). Cut into twelve 7.5 cm (4 in) rounds and line the tins. Next, put 10g ($1/2$ oz) apple purée into each tart and then top up with the filling.

For the filling

175 g (6 oz) caster sugar
175 g (6 oz) butter (soft)
175 g (6 oz) ground rice
$1^1/2$ tsp almond essence
2 eggs separated

Whisk together the sugar and butter until pale and fluffy before adding the egg yolks and ground rice. Whisk in the egg whites and spoon the mixture onto the top of the apple purée in each of the tarts. Bake for 25 minutes at 200°C/400°F/gas mark 6.

Paul's Mum's saffron buns

(makes 15)

450 g (1 lb) strong plain flour
25 g (1 oz) fresh yeast
120 g (4 oz) clotted cream
50 g (2 oz) caster sugar
50 g (2 oz) sultanas
50 g (2 oz) currants
150 ml (5 fl oz) milk
150 ml (5 fl oz) water
1/2 tsp salt
1/4 tsp nutmeg (freshly grated)
1/4 tsp mixed spice
1/4 tsp cinnamon
sachet of saffron

Begin by boiling the water and adding to it the saffron. Leave to stand for 10 minutes before pouring in the cold milk to reduce the temperature. Add this liquid mixture to the yeast.

In a large mixing bowl sieve the flour, salt and spices, add the cream and fruit, and now mix in the yeast liquid. Knead together for 2–3 minutes. Cover with cling film, wrap in a clean tea towel and leave 'to prove' in a warm place for 1 hour or until the mixture has doubled in size.

Grease a baking tray and divide into 15 equal size buns, moulding with your fingers as if you were making bread buns. Cover again with a clean tea towel and leave to prove for another 30 minutes.

Bake in a preheated oven (190°C/375°F/gas mark 5) for 15–20 minutes.

Preserves

Fiery green tomato chutney

You will need eight 450 g (1 lb) jars

- 1.35 kg (3 lb) green tomatoes (quartered)
- 1.1 kg (2 lb 8 oz) onions (chopped)
- 1 kg (2 lb 2 oz) prepared Cox's eating apples (peeled, quartered and cored)
- 4 cloves of garlic (crushed)
- 5 red chillies (roughly chopped)
- 25 g (1 oz) root ginger (crushed)
- $^1/_2$ tbsp cayenne pepper
- 25 g (1 oz) mustard seeds
- 700 g (1 lb 8 oz) demerara sugar
- 1.75 l (3 pt) red wine vinegar
- 2 level tsp salt

Place the prepared tomatoes, onions and apples into a preserving pan with the mustard seeds, cayenne pepper, salt and half the vinegar. Tie the crushed garlic, ginger and roughly chopped chillies in a piece of muslin and drop in the pan. Bring to the boil and simmer for 30 minutes, stirring now and then. Add the sugar and remaining vinegar, and bring back to simmering point. Gently simmer for approximately 1 hour or until the chutney has thickened – don't forget to stir from time to time towards the end of cooking, as it tends to stick a little.

Pour your chutney into warmed, sterilised jars, and seal and label. Store for at least 2 months (if you can!) before eating.

Three coloured pepper relish

(makes four 350g (12oz) jars)

4 red peppers (washed, deseeded and sliced thinly)
4 yellow peppers (washed, deseeded and sliced thinly)
4 green peppers (washed, deseeded and sliced thinly)
2 red chillies (washed, deseeded and sliced thinly)
110g (4oz) cooking apples (peeled, cored and chopped)
1 large onion (chopped)
175g (6oz) soft brown sugar
570ml (1pt) malt vinegar
$^1/_4$ tsp cayenne pepper
1 tsp salt
2 cloves of garlic (crushed)

Place all the ingredients except the sugar and 275ml ($^1/_2$pt) vinegar into a preserving pan and simmer for 20 minutes. Then add the sugar and remaining vinegar, and simmer for another 20 minutes until all the vinegar has been absorbed. Pour into sterilised jars and seal. This relish keeps for six months and goes well with cold meat or cheese.

Lemon and lavender jelly

(makes two 350g/12oz jars)

rind and juice of 6 lemons
make up to 570ml (1pt) with cold water
450g (1lb) preserving sugar
12 sprigs of lavender

Place all the ingredients into a saucepan and bring to the boil over a gentle heat until all the sugar has dissolved. Then boil rapidly for 5 minutes. Test in the same way as for the cider apple jelly (see page 38), strain through a very fine sieve and pour into two warmed, sterilised jars.

Cider apple and ginger jelly

There is no need to peel or core the apples for this recipe. Makes approximately 1.3 kg (3 lb) of jelly.

2 kg (4 lb 4 oz) cider apples (washed and quartered)
1.1 l (2 pt) water
450 g (1 lb) preserving sugar and 110 g (4 oz) crushed fresh
  ginger for every 570 ml (1 pt) of juice

Put the apples and water into a fairly large pan and bring to the boil. Then simmer for 15–20 minutes or until the apples have reduced to a pulp. Pour the pulp into a jelly bag or muslin, and leave to strain for several hours – this is best done the day before the jelly-making proper.

Put two saucers into the fridge to help with testing the jelly. Measure out the strained liquid and add the sugar and ginger. Over a low heat gently dissolve the sugar, then boil rapidly for 5 minutes. Take off the heat and test the jelly – drop a little liquid onto a saucer, push it gently with the edge of your finger and if it wrinkles it's ready to pot; if it doesn't, boil for another 5 minutes and try again (this method applies to all jelly and preserve making).

Once ready, pour into warmed, sterilised jars and seal. A small cup, plastic measuring jug or jam funnel is helpful in filling the jars without too many spills.

Spicy bottled organic pears

1 kg (2 lb 2 oz) firm William pears
350 g (12 oz) demerara sugar
275 ml (¹/₂ pt) red wine vinegar
275 ml (¹/₂ pt) scrumpy
2 small cinnamon sticks or 1 large stick (broken into
    3 or 4 pieces)
¹/₂ orange cut into slices
10 whole cloves
10 juniper berries
10 black peppercorns

Peel the pears, halve and core them, and place in a bowl of cold water with a squeeze of lemon juice to stop them turning brown. Put all the other ingredients into a large saucepan on a low heat and bring to the boil slowly, stirring until all the sugar has dissolved.

Drain the pears and discard the water, then add them to the saucepan and simmer for 20 minutes or until they are tender. Take off the heat, strain carefully through a sieve and put the pears into the preserving jar. Boil the syrup for 6 minutes or until it has reduced to 425 ml (³/₄ pt) and pour onto the pears – cover completely and make sure the orange slices, cinnamon sticks and spices are included. Cover tightly and store for around 6 weeks in a cool dark place. You can then serve these pears with cold meats or cheese or, even better, they are fabulous served warm with home-made vanilla ice cream.

Index